Sebastian's Roo

Hide and Seek

by Erin Kochakji

Illustrated by Nadine McLaughlin

Graphics North

Jay NY USA

Graphics North
PO Box 218
Jay, New York 12941

Library of Congress Control Number: pbx42274

ISBN: 978-0-692-79724-2

Book and cover design by Nadine McLaughlin
Back Cover Photo by: Brenda Green

Illustrations by: Nadine McLaughlin

To Jesus, who invites us all
to be like little children.

To Mom,
whose love and generosity
are endless.

To Sebastian's Roo's:
Savannah and Sierra.

And in loving memory of Sebastian,
a faithful companion forever.

From
Brenda Green and Erin Kochakji

Sebastian's Roo

I'm sure you've heard
some people say,

"A dog is
man's best friend."

But man is not the only one
on whom we dogs
depend.

A dog's love reaches very far:
to those
both big
and small.

And dogs like me
have hearts *so big*
there's room enough
for all.

And just like owners
name their pets,
we pets
can pick names
too.

So,
let me introduce you
to my friend—
I named her

"Roo."

My Roo,
she loves me
even when
my fur may be unruly

and doesn't squirm away from
doggy kisses
that are

d r$_{oo}$ly.

And in return for that,
a watchful eye
I always keep,

to make sure Roo
is safe and sound ...

... even when
asleep.

But in the day,
it's time to play!
Her favorite?
Hide and seek.

I'll hear her say,
"You must obey!
Sebastian, do *not peek!*"

Then off she runs
to pick the perfect spot
in which to crouch;

... and when I hear
my Roo's command,

I head straight for
the couch.

I'm pretty sure that
by itself,
a pillow doesn't jiggle;

and last time
that I checked,
I swore that sofas
do not

giggle.

But, if you have
a Roo like mine,
you must
know how to play

and not let on
and spoil the fun
or
give it all
away!

Perhaps,
I'll take
a few more laps
and sniff along the floor.

(I'll have her wait
    until she just can't
        take it anymore.)

And when,
at last,
she smiles and says,

"Sebastian,

I love you..."

I hope she knows my

Roo... roo...

roooooooo

just means:

I

love you

too !

ROO‑'ROO‑'ROO

Made in the USA
Monee, IL
08 September 2021